High Functioning Autistic Spectrum Disorder: 50 Rules For A Happy Life

From a Mother Who Loves You Lots

Dedication

My dearest Gabriel,

This book is dedicated to you, my beloved son. Without you, it would never have been written.

From the moment that you were born, I felt a bond form between us that would last longer than our own lives. When I first saw your face, I knew that things would never be the same again. It was only when you were diagnosed with autism that I appreciated how different they would really be.

I must admit that I was scared. I was worried for the future and stuck thinking about the past. I would often sit and wonder whether there was something I could have done to prevent it, or whether I was to blame for it. Meanwhile, my fears for the future were growing each day.

I want you to know that Mommy was wrong to ever think this way and that you should never see autism as something that is holding you back. I wish I realised sooner that I was looking in the wrong places. Instead of thinking about the past or worrying about the future, it was the present moment that I should have paid attention to much earlier on.

I have watched you grow into a wonderful man, with good values and a mind sharper than most. Nothing ever went wrong. You are the best thing to have happened to us in our lives and your autism is nothing but one of your many gifts from God.

We are all different. We all think differently, we all act differently and we all serve a different purpose in life. **I realised quickly that there is no such thing as normal. If there was, there wouldn't be a single normal person on earth.**

You are your own person, and your autism is a small part of the amazing human being that you are. Embrace it, but never let it define you! You are many things other than what you have been diagnosed with. Share your gifts and always believe in yourself, for you are capable of anything you put your mind and heart to. I know that you will find your own version of success if you have that belief and follow your heart.

Keep doing what you love and always ask God for guidance. This book is something I want to leave behind for you, if I am ever not close by when you need me. But know that you are never alone when it comes to seeking help.

I have written this from my heart, and I know deep down that with reflection and thought you will understand me and put these things into practice.

Always remember that my love for you is a million times greater than the universe itself!

Much love,

Mommy

xxx

Prologue

The purpose of this book is to leave a legacy for my beloved son, Gabriel, who has High Functioning Autistic Spectrum Disorder. This legacy contains rules that will hopefully help him survive in this life journey.

Have you heard of Autistic Spectrum Disorder? Do you have anyone in your family or know someone who has it?

If yes, then I sincerely hope that you will be able to relate to any of the content mentioned. My aim is to provide a shared humanity for anyone experiencing ASD, whether it is themselves or through a family member.

If the answer is no, then I hope it gives you an awareness of what an ASD person can face with and I thank you for reading this book.

Finally, I hope you will be able to apply the rules (whether you are autistic or not) in your life to guide you.

So let's begin…

It was nearing the end of my lunch break that I sat at the local café, finishing off the last of my food. I was staring vacantly at the door when a mother and son walked in. The boy looked about 9 years old, with brown skin and dark hair covering his eyes, although he latched onto this mother like a child half his age. The pair queued at the till for a few minutes, until they made it to the front to place their order. It was then that the boy erupted into tears.

"Chips!" he shouted. "I want chips!"

After many lunch breaks spent at this café, I knew full well that chips were not on the menu. As the lady tried to explain this to her child, the kid's tantrum only got worse. As they ordered, waited and even once the food had arrived, the howling would not stop.

Soon enough, scalding looks were being thrown in the way of the mother, who hid shamefully behind her headscarf. The atmosphere in the café had suddenly changed and within minutes, the noise prompted people to leave.

It was at this point that I too got up and left. I walked briskly through the cafeteria doors, just like the customers before me. But unlike them, it was not the noise that drove me out.

Making my way to the McDonalds nearby, I found my colleague waiting in line, quickly explained what I was doing and cut the queue. I placed my order and ran straight back to the cafeteria, arriving to see the place emptier than when I left it with the child's cries still filling the air.

I approached the worn-out mother who was attempting to feed her son the sandwich they had ordered, rested my palm on her shoulder gently and with my other hand and offered over a brown paper bag to the boy. The child looked at me confused, his shyness now covering his temper.

"Go on." I said encouragingly, with a warm smile across my face "Open it." The boy hesitantly peered into the opening of the bag, only to find a red cardboard box, filled with hot golden fries.

The mother then spoke, her words heavy and tired; "Please, you didn't have to. I am sorry about the noise. My son has autism."

I smiled again; this time a smile of understanding and empathy. "My son has autism, too." I said reassuringly. "He's 18 now and all grown up!" I saw the face of that lady changed and suddenly there was comfort and hope in her eyes.

There are parents and carers all over the world who had similar experiences to us, surrounded by others who can't ever truly understand. More importantly, there are the people with autism themselves, who are often the most misunderstood.

It is only with love, care and support that a person with ASD can learn to deal effectively with the often chaotic and unpredictable world around them but it is often difficult for the people who care for them to let go and allow their loved ones to take on the world by themselves.

Should anyone find themselves in these pages, I want to thank you for taking the time to read what I have written. Although written with my son as the primary audience, this book applies to the many other people out there with High Functioning ASD. I have written the majority of the book in a way that I hope a large proportion of individuals with High Functioning ASD can understand, however the guide is written largely for the parents or carers of those with the condition, so that they may translate these rules appropriately to the person they are caring for.

I have broken these ideas and lessons down into a form that is short, sweet and easy to understand for anybody. Whether you have autism yourself, someone close to you may have it or if you're just reading this out of curiosity, you can view these rules in a way that they will still apply.

Autistic or not – we're all people just figuring out this weird and wonderful thing called life and we can all benefit from this set of helpful tips and rules. I trust that each person who reads this book has a beautifully different way of thinking and whoever you may be, I hope you all find guidance and wisdom in what I have written.

As the name suggests, autism is a spectrum – colourful and varied; a rainbow of talents and traits that make each and every person with ASD special in their own way. I understand that this means the book can only appeal to so many people and so I encourage parents and carers to read it themselves so they can interpret and teach it as they see fit, if necessary.

I hope you take in the following lessons – try and implement them into your life or teach someone (with or without autism) to do so in theirs. In this book, I try to present ideas that one could take basic life principles and practice them in their own right, with the hope of providing some facility to dealing with everyday issues connected to autism. Good luck – and remember that practice makes perfect!

CONTENTS

PART ONE: RULES AND GUIDANCE FOR DEALING WITH YOURSELF

Rule #1: Be True To Yourself (It's As Easy As ABC)

I thought long and hard about what I would write as the first rule in this guide. In the end I decided; it is to be true to who you are.

When I was in primary school, I had a set of friends who were twins. Although they looked and sounded similar, they had very different personalities. Even those of us that are somewhat identical have differences, because no two people are the same. We are all unique in our own way. Realise that you are one of a kind and that to be yourself is as easy as ABC:

A is for **Accepting** yourself

Once you accept the things that make you who you are, you will find peace in your heart. Accepting your situation is one of the best things you can do to move forward. If you accept that other people will be different how they think, behave and operate then you will find your peace of mind.

Why will accepting that you are different give you peace? It is because you will learn to not resent people who do not understand you. When you resent someone, you can feel bitter and annoyed at them. If you have already accepted that they just see things differently because of how they were made, then there is no need to get annoyed! It is not your fault or theirs – it's just how life works!

Accepting differences is good, but it does not mean that you should not try and make yourself understood or stop trying to understand others. Whether one has autism or not, they can struggle to be understood. If you try to understand, it will help to prepare you to be someone who can accept other people as well as yourself.

If you still find that you can't understand, don't get annoyed with yourself. Be kind to yourself. Pat yourself on the back and say "Well done! I am doing well to understand others who may not think like me." Accept that you think differently and move on.

B is for **Belief** (in yourself)

Henry Ford famously said, "Whether you think you can or think you can't, you are right."

Remember that what you believe tends to come true! You must believe in yourself and your ability. If you don't, then how can you expect other people to believe in you?

Believing in yourself means you trust yourself to do the things that you are trying to do, even if those things may seem like they are too difficult to be done. Always give yourself some words of encouragement and you will be more likely to achieve what you want and be the person you want to become. Tell yourself things such as:

"I am capable of doing this!"
"I can do anything I put my mind to!"
"I will get this done because I know I can!"

Once you do this small thing, you are nearly all the way there!

C is for **Character** Development

When you're thinking of the hero in a comic book, what is it that makes that character good?

Part of being true to yourself is developing the hero that you already. A good heroic character is someone who:

- Helps those in need or less fortunate
- Is humble when they achieve great things
- Does not hurt people to get to their success
- Help others without expecting something in return
- Is remembered even long after they are gone
- Acknowledges their weaknesses, tries to improve on them and learns how to play to their strengths.

Your character says a lot about who you are as a person, so make sure you always try to create a good one. The villain in the comic tends to chase all the money and power in the world but always finds themselves unloved and defeated at the end of the story. Therefore, remember to be yourself by accepting the things that make you different, believing in your abilities and developing your character to unleash the hero that you are.

Rule #2: Don't Compare Yourself To Others – You Are Good Enough

Albert Einstein, the face of intelligence, once said:

"Everybody is a genius. But if you judge a fish by its ability to climb a tree, it will live its whole life believing that it is stupid."

What did he mean? He meant that a fish and a monkey are good at different things. In the same way you may be better than others at certain things.

You cannot say that a monkey is a better animal because he can climb, because the fish is better than the monkey at swimming. **In the same way, someone may be better than you when it comes to socialising or doing mental maths but you may be more logical, creative or artistic than they are**. Be happy and content for who you are and realise you have something special to offer the world. Have a good self-esteem. Remember that you are good enough.

Rule #3: Look After Yourself (Self-Love)

What is self-love and more importantly, why should you love yourself?

Self-love isn't the same as being selfish or self-interested. It means forgiveness and respect for yourself as a human being. You do it because to love oneself results in the following:

- When you make a mistake, you forgive yourself. You say, "it's okay. I am only human. I forgive myself and learn the lesson from this mistake."
- Looking after your own well-being. Are you eating and sleeping well? Make sure you find time to relax and ease your mind. How? Meditation (few minutes of deep breathing a day). You can do this by having some quiet time in the bathroom, even just for a few minutes. Remember to close the door and close off any outside noise as much as possible.
- **When you love and look after yourself, you will have the ability to help others.**

Rule #4: Have Confidence In Yourself (Self-Esteem)

It is important for you to maintain a good self-esteem. What is it? Put simply, self-esteem it is how much value you give yourself. It is how proud you are to be you.

When you have good self-esteem, you are more likely to succeed. Being diagnosed with autism should not impact this self-esteem. You should be confident in what makes you different and appreciate yourself. This doesn't mean that you should be arrogant. Arrogance is being so proud that you start to show-off. Instead, try to appreciate the things that make you special so that you can live your life positively.

All human beings tend to talk to themselves in a way that is negative. Imagine this as a cartoon devil on your shoulder. At the same time, there is an angel on your other shoulder feeding you words that give you confidence and make you happy. Try to learn to ignore the negative self-talk and listen more to the positive thoughts about yourself. Ignore that devilish cartoon version of yourself and listen carefully to the angel that assures you and tells you to be happy.

Rule #5: Be Your Own Best Friend, But NOT Your Only One!

You often say to me; "Mommy, most of the time, I would rather be alone than mingle with others."

Great! That means you know how to enjoy your own company! When you do certain things alone, you tend to be in complete control and can choose to do what you like. When with others, you often have to consider what they like. **Enjoying your own company is a bit of time to love yourself and treat yourself as your own best friend.**

But don't forget – there are times that being with others can really help you! There are times that you will have to be with others. Having a good relationship with other people is important because it means you can get the love and help you need from others. It also serves as good practice to be social so that you can have a strong bond between other people who can care for you and give you company when you feel like it's time to be social.

The main thing to remember is, when you decide to be with others, enjoy being with them and don't wish that you are alone!

Rule #6: Learn From Mistakes, Forgive Yourself and Move On

When you were growing up, you would often get upset with yourself if you made a mistake. Recognising the mistake is important, but what is more important is how you choose to act after the mistake has been made. Once you feel you have done something wrong:

1. Be honest with yourself and accept that it was the wrong thing to do
2. Think about why the mistake has happened – what caused it?
3. Think about what you will do/improve in the future to not make that mistake again
4. Forgive yourself and move on, trying to be mindful of not making the mistake again

The last step (forgiveness) is important as it means you are ready to move on. Everybody makes mistakes – we are all human! It is only the best people who learn from them.

Just to help this method make a bit more sense, I'll give you an example you can remember of how to apply those four rules in the best way possible.

I suffer from dry eyes and always manage to keep my medication on hand. It was at your uncle's wedding last year (a very important and exciting occasion) when I made the mistake of not taking the little bottle of eye-drops with me. We were already in the cab when I realised that I left it at home! I was lucky enough on that day to find that your auntie carried around a similar bottle for herself, which I used to relieve the discomfort.

Instead of becoming annoyed at myself for forgetting something important and potentially ruining my experience of a special day, I followed the four steps outlined above. Below is how I used them:

1. **I was honest with myself** and realised that I should be more mindful about carrying my medication.
2. **I thought about why** I did not have my medication on hand and realised it was because I was distracted, excited and in a rush.
3. I realised that it was important to always check my bag before I leave and pay attention to the few things that were important to me **in the future**.
4. **I forgave myself** and told myself I'd do better next time.

I don't regret making any of the mistakes I made in my life - big or small. I don't regret them because I forgave myself and turned those mistakes into lessons that I could learn from in the future - lessons that have made me the better person I am today. When you find yourself making mistakes, remember to also do the same.

Rule #7: Relax Your Mind When Doing Difficult Things

Your teachers have always said that you participate well in class when you are not stressed out. Although a little pressure and motivation is good, I find that learning is best when your mind is settled and relaxed. How do you get yourself relaxed?

If you use that amazing imagination of yours, it will happen easily! Imagine yourself relaxed and believe it or not, you will become whatever is in your head. Do some deep breathing for few minutes when you feel anxious and find a space that is comfortable for you to be in. We'll get on more to meditation and breathing in the next rule.

You have always been very chilled out. When you notice I am getting anxious, you even say to me "Mum, calm down." When you are nervous, it can be seen by the people around you. If you are able to notice when I am like that, think about how important it is to stay calm and collected around other people who will notice things in you.

When it comes to facing your fears, a relaxed mindset is the best thing to have. Before your blood tests, you used to always tell me that you were scared of needles. Most people are! You always have the option to panic and worry about the needle, thinking long and hard about pain, but like the nurse said – it's just a scratch. When I asked you to relax your mind and think of calming things, you barely noticed that the needle was used! My point is that, **when you relax your mind, your body will do the same.** Apply this technique whenever you feel anxious or stressed out. **Remember that your mind is yours and only you have the power to control it!**

The next rule will help with teaching you how to be relaxed when dealing with pressured situations.

Rule #8: Meditate

You might wonder, "How do you meditate?" - Trust me; it isn't something that's difficult to do. In fact, it is practically one of the easiest things you can try and do.

1. Close your eyes and find somewhere comfortable
2. Breathe deeply and slowly, in and out, listening to your breaths
3. Imagine that when you breathe out, you are letting go of all the things that are worrying you and that when you breathe in, you are inhaling clean and fresh blue air
4. Listen to the sound of your breathing and let this be what you are focusing on
5. Do this for 3 to 5 minutes each day, or whenever you are feeling stressed.

Meditation, where you sit in peace and quiet, is a very good habit to have so that you can clear your head and relax your body. Try to do this twice a day, once in the morning and once in the evening. It will only take few minutes of your time but it will be good for your mental well being.

Rule #9: Take Your Time

People do things at different speeds. Some people can move quickly while others move slower. The truth is that doing something too fast can lead to silly mistakes. You have to do things at a speed that you are comfortable with and not worry about anybody else. Practice the type of relaxing I just mentioned when you are carrying out tasks, as this makes you less likely to rush, more likely to focus and prevent you from making errors. It is always better to move forward slowly than end up moving backwards because you fell backwards trying to move so fast.

Rule #10: Face Your Fears (But Always Practice Caution)

This rule focuses on doing the things that are difficult and may scare you, but also being careful when you do them.

Why should we face our fears? Because sometimes we irrationally fear things that may be good for us and can help us grow. By being brave and doing things that challenge us, we can become better people.

When you were about 4 years old, I told your Dad that I wanted to take you to Spain for 4 nights, just you and me. He stopped whatever he was doing and asked - "Are you sure?" I responded with "Yes! I have booked the tickets already!" I won't ever forget the look on his face. I understood his surprise. At the time, a trip to the supermarket alone would make me worried. I would always glue myself to you, scared that you'd stumble somewhere unfamiliar and be taken from me. As silly as it sounds – it's the truth.

Whenever we left the house, I would squat down to your eye level and say sternly, "Stick around with Mommy and Daddy and don't talk to strangers!" There was never a response – just an angelic little face looking back at me.

In the end, I did it. I took you abroad without your Dad and stepped out of my comfort zone. And guess what? We both survived! After that, I learned to trust myself taking you to new and exciting places without getting too worried. It was taking that big step that allowed me to let you be more independent and experience more of life.

I must admit I didn't sleep much during the holiday, but it was worth it! I learned that the only way to combat your fears is to act against them. But practice caution! If you were afraid of snakes, would you wrestle one? Of course not!

Make sure you are sensible and that the action you take is not something that will harm you, but something that will help you grow. If the fear is stopping you from doing what you love, you should try and confront it!

Rule #11: Count Your Blessings and Be Grateful For What You Have

It is easy to compare yourself to others, or to start thinking about all the things you don't have but whenever you begin to feel that you are lacking in something, start counting your blessings.

Always try to be thankful for what you have rather than to focus on what you don't. Remember that you can see with your eyes and hear with your ears. Remember that, whether you find it difficult or not, you can talk and can try to understand others. Remember that you have a family that loves you and people who can care for you. Remember that you have your health and your life and your home.

All these things are things you should be grateful for, because not everybody has them. Even the smallest things, such as the sun in your face, the air you breathe and the water you drink should not be taken for granted. **Life itself is a gift and be thankful you are alive to experience it.** When you start to focus on what you don't have, share time with people who are less fortunate than you are. Give food and charity to the poor, or help the old frail lady cross the street. Doing this is not only a kind and noble thing to do, it will allow you to think about the struggles of others and make you feel better about the gifts you have been given in life.

Rule #12: Search For Your Own Version Of Success

You have said that you have always been interested in making a graphic novel. If that's the case, then keep practising until you can do it! Many people in the world wake up each morning to do something they don't enjoy doing and have no time to follow their dreams. Always make time for your dreams and put your heart into them, that way you will be more likely to succeed.

When you are climbing the ladder of success and trying to obtain your goals, ensure you are not hurting others along the way. Don't take shortcuts or ask anybody to do the work for you. Instead, have the guts to do it on your own. If you do this, you can stand tall in the knowledge that you reached success because of your own hard work, commitment and dedication!

Always focus on your goal and your passion but remember that you have the freedom to change your mind if you have a change of heart. Don't commit to something you do not love, but never give up on the things that you do love.

Rule #13: Learn How To Deal With Failure

Failure is part of life as much as success. It's not only humans that fail, even "perfect" computers crash and malfunction. When failure happens to you, don't let it define you. Take it on the chin, learn from it and move on.

When I was much younger, I was working as a secretary and saw a job opportunity that would have given me nearly double what I was earning. Without hesitation, I grabbed the opportunity and applied, only thinking about the money. I spent three months in that job in what is called a "probation period", where they try you out to see if you can handle the work. Unfortunately, after that amount of time, despite how hard I worked, I did not pass. It was a knock to my confidence to realise that I had failed to keep a better paying job but instead of giving up, I learned from it and realised that I did not have enough experience before going into it. I promised myself that I would be more prepared if another opportunity like this came my way and didn't let the failure stop me.

When you fail, learn why you failed and prepare for the future, rather than being discouraged. Be proud that you at least tried and learn your lesson from it. If you've learned something, then you have won. It is important to always be resilient in life. **Resilience is dealing with life's difficulties by fighting back and carrying on.** It is not stopping when you meet an obstacle or a failure, but instead pushing through, being patient and trying harder. Build up your resilience so that you can take on any of life's difficulties!

Even more than this, resilience is making the most out of a bad situation. Like our priest once said in his sermon, "you can't have a perfect day all of the time. When things go wrong, try and generate goodness out of it". **Looking for the good things in a bad situation is the same as finding the lessons in your failures.** The bigger the failure, the bigger the lesson and the more you get out of a bad situation.

Rule #14: Always Have a Plan B

Having a plan B is like having a spare tyre. If one of the wheels of your car blows out on the motorway, always have another in the back to replace it so you can keep moving forward. If you don't have that spare tyre, you will be stuck in the road for a long time.

Let's think of an example of where a plan B can come in handy:

You are travelling around London and you have lost your oyster card. Do you panic? No!

- Plan **B**: You have had the initiative to bring cash with you so you can pay for a ticket to go home.
- Plan **C**: You also have your bank card which you can use for travel.
- Plan **D**: In the worst-case scenario, you can call your Dad and he can pick you up.

Another example is if you lose your keys to your front door.

- Plan **B**: There's no need to worry if you know that someone will be home to let you in.
- Plan **C**: If there isn't, you can get the spare key you keep in one of your neighbours or auntie's house.
- Plan **D**: In the worst-case scenario, you can stay at the home of somebody you know and trust and call the locksmith so he can help you in the next day.

Here - you can see that having multiple back up plans ensure you don't find yourself stuck in difficult situations and that you are always safe. You can apply this to bigger things in life as well, such as your career.

Rule #15: "Don't Sweat the Small Stuff"

"Don't Sweat the Small Stuff" (Carlson, 1997) was one of the best books I have read. The message that Dr Carlson tried to convey is that life is too short to be annoyed by the little things. Although this is easier said than done, he was absolutely right. There is no point getting stressed out by petty things in life – all it does is slow you down and make you anxious. It is better to be happy and practice that resilience we talked about – moving on despite difficulty. There is no time to obsess over the tiny little mishaps in our lives!

Carlson, R. (1997). Don't sweat the small stuff--and its all small stuff. New York: Hyperion.

Rule #16: Don't Major in Minor

Much like the previous rule, this one focuses on ensuring that you do not preoccupy yourself with small things that take up a lot of your time. It is easy to get distracted with TV and video games, but there are so many other things that can be done to give you a bigger sense of personal fulfilment, such as finishing your graphic novel!

I had a friend in college who would always spend her revision week cleaning her house. She would dust the doors and wash the rugs and degrease the oven, all the while the most important thing she should have been doing was revising for her exams. Cleaning your house is a good thing to do, but there is a time and place for it and that is not during exam week.

Unlike my friend, focus on the most important task first and learn to prioritise. The oven can be cleaned any time but the exams have to be revised for now! **Learn to not waste time on the small things and focus on the things that matter most.**

Rule #17: Practice Mindfulness In Everything You Do

There is beauty and importance in everything you are doing. When you wake up in the morning, you can appreciate the fact that God has given you another day on earth. When you brush your teeth, you can think carefully about how you are cleaning them, what the toothpaste tastes like and how it ended up on your toothbrush. When you take a shower, you can feel the water against your skin and be grateful and curious about how it got from nature through the pipes and into your home. **Everything you do has meaning behind it.**

When you do things, try to not forget about the meaning or you will not enjoy the experience fully. When you multitask or do things too quickly, you can easily lose sight of the beauty and importance of what you are doing.

For example, imagine you are eating your favourite ice cream, chatting on the phone to your friend and searching for your keys. It wouldn't be a good idea to do all three at the same time, though. You will be less likely to understand what your friend is saying and appreciate the conversation you are having over the phone. You will be less likely to fully taste and savour your favourite ice cream and enjoy it as a treat. On top of this, you will be less mindful of where you last left your keys and whether or not you are looking in the correct places.

If you are mindful and choose to do things one at a time, you will begin to enjoy each experience more or get better results from what you are doing. This is because your mind is focused on the single task at hand and not distracted by several other things. Be mindful, not mindless.

Rule #18: Follow Your Instinct

Following your instinct is good when you are trying to make quick decisions. Instinct or intuition is also known as 'gut feeling.' It is the feeling you get when your body tells you something is right or wrong. In reality, instinct is the result of lots of quick estimates and calculations in your brain that try and guess correct answers and a lot of the time this guessing is quite accurate.

Instinct is also coupled with initiative. Initiative is a word that means your ability to assess things and act in the right way. If you picked up this book because you felt lost and needed advice, you took the initiative to pick it up and start reading it. You are finding something that can help you in a difficult situation or help you in the future.

I can remember a while back, when you were doing your final art project, that I thought about backing up your work on our home PC. I never asked you in the end and two months later, all of your documents became corrupted. It was my instinct and intuition that told me to make the back-up and there were consequences to me ignoring them.

Most of the time, your instinct is right and there are hundreds of situations where you can use both instinct and initiative, at home, college and work. Here are a few more examples:

- Collecting your laundry from the garden when you feel that it might rain.
- Offering to do the hoovering when Daddy seems tired.
- Doing your homework when you feel you might not have time later.
- Offering your seat to a person on the bus if they seem to have difficulty standing.

Rule #19: Take Action To Defeat Procrastination

Human beings can get lazy and have the tendency to put things off. Sometimes you look at a task that you know you should be doing now and instead start to convince yourself, "Maybe I'll get that done later…"

Your brain is good at making up stories as to why you shouldn't get important things done. Don't give it the chance. When you start to feel lazy and want to put things off for later, recognise this and set yourself a three second timer in your head. After three seconds, shoot up from your bed or sofa (or wherever you may be perched) and get to work! Explode with energy and get the task done! The more you think about doing something, the more likely you will convince yourself not to, the more tired you will get and the less likely you will do it in the end.

What about bigger tasks that can't be done as quickly? When trying to write this book, I procrastinated a lot at first. In the end, I knew that it would not be written on its own and so I set myself the target of writing at least 200 words a day. If I felt like doing more once I sat down, then I would and with time the first draft was completed and ready to be edited. People tend to say that if you're going to eat an elephant, you have to do it one bite at a time. Big tasks can seem challenging at first, much like the idea of having to eat an elephant whole, so it is important you set yourself targets and break up the task into little pieces.

At the end of the day, you reap what you sow. This means that whatever seeds you plant, you can collect the produce from. **If you do the work, you can collect the results.** If you choose to lie to yourself and put things off, then there will be no reward.

Rule #20: It's Never Too Late To Make a Change

You should never underestimate your ability to make changes in your life for the better. These changes can happen no matter how young or old, rich or poor, fit or fat you are. **There is no such thing as being "too late" to change something.**

Why? Because at the end of the day, you are in control of your behaviour. You are in control of your thoughts and your actions. Saying you can't do something because you're too old is just an excuse that you are telling yourself. Colonel Sanders, the man who franchised KFC, was in his 60s when he made his dreams come true. He turned his life around and did something great for himself and his loved ones. If you ever feel there are things in your life that you could improve or do better, work on them! Don't make excuse and don't let yourself believe that it is too late. Keep practising, working at it and focusing on your goals. Nobody else is going to do it for you.

Rule #21: Use Your Own Judgement

In this world, there will be many critics everywhere. They criticise anything – things, people, the government and the list goes on. They may be experts in their own field but do not listen to them. Use your own judgment, find out yourself and then make a decision based on your own experiences.

I love watching horror and action films. Once, I watched a film that was given a 3 star rating. I watched it regardless of the rating and soon found out that the film actually gave a very good moral lesson and for me that I think it deserved at least 4 stars.

You want to read a particular book but critics say it is rubbish? Find out yourself by reading and deciding for yourself. Always use your own judgement.

Do you have a colleague that is not popular because they are shy and introverted? Speak to them anyway. If they respond to you, that is great. If they do not, at least you tried. Try not to be offended if the person does not respond enthusiastically. It could be that the person is really shy and wants to be alone.

Just remember that critics are being paid for one thing – to criticise. Don't let them influence your decision.

Rule #22: Find Peace and Solitude Away From Your Screen

When I was a child, I spent a large amount of my time climbing trees, swimming in rivers and playing into the night with the kids in my neighbourhood. I grew up in a time when there were no mobile phones, tablets or laptops. It was much simpler back then and I learned to appreciate nature and be present in the world around me. Now, I find that our lives are dominated by technology that is constantly evolving. Although we are fortunate enough to benefit from these advances, it is easy to become slaves to our devices. Modern day gadgets give us a never-ending stimulus that keeps us away from enjoying the real world around us.

I remember when we went to Greece and sat in a restaurant as a family, observing the couple sitting opposite our table. They were physically so close to each other, yet they were also so far apart. I could tell that neither of them paid attention to the other. Instead, their faces were both lit up by the blue light of their phones. I found it interesting to observe these two, as they tapped and swiped away, not ever stopping to say a word to each other. The very fact that I noticed this was because I, myself, chose not to go on my phone.

By giving yourself a break from technology, you find the time to savour the beauty of the world and notice things that you might miss. You give your eyes and your mind a well-earned rest and find peace and solitude with your time. When you wake up from sleep or get home after a long day, be brutal. Resist the urge to waste time on your phone. Turn it off and find other ways to relax, either by reading or meditating or drawing. Do the work you need to get done, find the space to rest your mind and gather your thoughts and then treat yourself occasionally to your phone. When enough time is spent on your device, then switch it back off again.

Spending less time in front of a screen means spending more time surrounded by nature. Explore your local park, river or lake. Take trips to the woods or the mountains. If there are none near to where you live, then even a small getaway anywhere that provides a chance to escape the everyday noise of modern life will suffice. Engage with nature as a tool to find yourself and you will achieve a state of calm and relaxation. You will feel much better inside.

Rule #23: Positive Thinking = Positive Feeling

I always say that energy goes straight from your head and to your heart. **Your thoughts become your feelings**. It is therefore essential that you monitor and control your way of thinking in order to have better control over how you feel. Negative thoughts fed straight into negative feelings and so it is important to develop a positive mental attitude.

In the words of Zig Ziglar, one of my favourite motivational speakers and authors, **"Your attitude and not your aptitude will determine your altitude."**

That's a lot of similar sounding words but what Zig Ziglar meant by that was that it is your behaviour and approach in life (**your attitude**) and not how clever or smart you are (**your aptitude**) that tells you how high up you will get in life (**your altitude**).

Positive thinking is not about ignoring or denying any hardships you may face on the journey towards your goal. Instead it is about **believing that you have the ability to reach that goal despite the challenges.** It focuses on the things we have talked about already; learning to deal with failure and believing in yourself. One way of positive thinking is simply by changing your cannots to cans. This is known as a "can-do attitude". Below are some examples of how to change your thoughts to become more positive.

Negative Thinking	**Can-do Attitude**
"I **can't** do it. It is **too hard** for me."	"I **can do it.** This will challenge me and my abilities."
"I **won't** be able to talk anyone in the party as I don't know those people."	"I **will** be able to talk to others in this party and might find people who share similar interests with me."
"It's my first day at work tomorrow and I **won't** know what to do."	"It's my first day at work tomorrow and **I will try** my best, but if I am struggling **I will seek advice** for things that I do not know."
"I **won't** ever be able to find a partner who will understand me."	"I **will** meet a person who will enjoy my company, appreciate who I am and show understanding towards the fact that I have autism."
"I **don't** think I can succeed in what I want to do."	"I **will** be successful in my chosen career if I am committed, hardworking and passionate."

Rule #24: Don't Rely On Memories Alone

People always say that we live life to make great memories, but we forget one simple thing: the fact that we forget! Our memory is a powerful thing; however, we cannot rely on it for everything. If I asked you what you were doing two years ago on this same date, would you be able to remember?

In order to look back at your life fully, it's important to document things. You can do this by taking pictures and storing them safely, or by using a diary or a small notebook to write anything important that you did on that day. Even the things that aren't very interesting are worth recording – you can look back and see how things have changed over time.

This does not mean you should be constantly recording or taking photos and looking at the world through the screen of your phone. It means that when you want to capture a moment, you should take a picture or two to remind you of that event. It means you should make a habit, before you go to bed each night, of writing your thoughts and feelings throughout the day. When you have the time, you can look through this journal and reflect on the ups and downs of life, either privately or through sharing them with those you love.

Rule #25: Less Is More

What do I mean by this? Firstly, I am saying that it is not good to have too much "stuff" around you. We live in a very materialistic society. What this means is that we are driven to have a lot of material things, such as money, clothes, toys, cars and video games. What happens is we end up focusing very little on the things that are non-material and give us happiness, such as family, love and peace.

Do not become a person who wants more and more. If you do, you will find your life becomes cluttered and difficult to manage. It is important to have the things you need, rather than lots of things you wanted at some point but will never use.

For example:

- If you have too many clothes, your wardrobe gets cluttered. Think of all the times you have given your clothes to charity because they no longer suit you. Instead, buy clothes that you know you love and will wear, rather than buying for the sake of it. Anything you don't use should be given away.
- If you have too many gadgets, your life gets filled with distractions. You will always want the next best thing and things that seemed new in the past will just take up space or be wasted as you hunt for the latest model. Instead, get gadgets that are reliable and look after them over time.
- If you acquire a lot of financial wealth, there might come a time where you may not know what to do with all of it. There are many rich and famous people that end up spending on the wrong things, such as drugs and other vices. Make sure you have an end goal of what you want to do with that newfound wealth before you go and acquire it!

"Less is more" can also relate to things that aren't physical, as you will find that it is never good to have too much of anything.

- Too much noise gives you a headache.
- Too much eating makes you fat.
- Too much confidence makes you seem big-headed.
- Too much socialising means not learning to be comfortable with your own company.
- Too much time alone means you can feel isolated.

Life is great when you learn to have just enough and never an excess. Those who are used to having too much will struggle to find happiness and find it difficult to appreciate the things that they do have. Getting down to just your basics and rewarding yourself with experiences (such as a holiday or a leisurely walk) rather than things is a far better way to live your life.

Rule #26: Use Your Eyes to See and Your Mouth to Smile

The first part of this rule is to use your eyes. This rule may seem silly, but a lot of the time it is something that people fail to do. Often, people tend to miss things by not looking hard enough.

One example of this is you have physically lost something. You might spend more time frantically rushing around the house and shouting for help than actually keeping your eyes peeled for what you are looking for. Instead, you should take a second to think about where it could be and look carefully for them.

In other situations, it is important to think first and observe before you act. Acting without assessing a situation can lead to you making mistakes. For example, you should try and decide whether someone looks tired or upset before you decide to speak to them, as this can influence how they respond to you.

As for your mouth, always aim to smile. You often tell me that you are uncomfortable smiling to people that you don't know. Forcing a smile can often feel unnatural, but even smiling to yourself as you walk down the street can make a difference to not only you but the people around you. **When you choose to smile, you tend to feel better and people tend to smile back.** It's human nature. The more you practice it, the easier it becomes and the more happiness you are spreading.

If a person chooses not to smile back, then don't take it personally. People have good days and bad days. You have tried your best and you shouldn't let it stop you from smiling and being friendly. A smile costs nothing, so give them out for free.

Rule #27: God Helps Those Who Help Themselves

I want to tell you about the power of prayer and how asking God for help can make a difference in your life. When you talk to God, or interact with something higher than yourself, you no longer feel alone and instead feel that someone is there to help, guide and protect you.

Asking God for help is the first step in doing difficult things that you may feel you are unable to accomplish. The next step is putting some of the burden on your own self. This means not sitting back and expecting miracles. It means working hard in the hope that God will make it easier for you rather than not doing anything in the hope that everything will magically happen.

For example, if you pray to pass your exams, you still need to revise to increase the chance to make it happen. Prayer may keep you calm in the exam room, or you might be lucky enough to stumble across some questions you know the answer to but if you have done no work and know nothing at all, how can you expect to pass? Remember that God will help those who ask for help but not everything will be done for you. You must help yourself first.

Rule #28: With Life There is Hope – Enjoy the Journey

It is often said that as long as you are alive there is still hope. After life, there is death and once your time is up, there is nothing you can do to help yourself or the world around you. Although life may get hard and you may encounter challenges along the way, always remember that you are still breathing. Remember that as long as this is the case, there is hope that things will get better and that you will grow to be better yourself. **Keep hope in your heart.**

They say that life is like a journey, filled with stops and diversions. Don't get annoyed when things go off track. We are all going to the same destination. We all die at some point. Until then, enjoy the view. Remember that visiting places you did not expect to visit is all part of the experience.

PART TWO: RULES AND GUIDANCE FOR DEALING WITH OTHERS

The first section of this rulebook was filled with advice on how to deal with and understand yourself. The next part of this book focuses mainly on how to deal with others in your daily life. It is one thing to understand yourself but understanding the people around you can be even more of a challenge. Whether you have autism or not, to relate to others means putting yourself in their shoes and using your imagination to perceive a situation. Hopefully with these rules, you will find it easier to do just that.

Rule #29: The Golden Rule - Treat Others How You Would Like to Be Treated

The Golden Rule is as follows: Treat others as you would like to be treated. Once you understand yourself more and have expectations of how others should respect you, you can then do the same for other people.

Ask yourself: Would you like other people to be rude to you?

If the answer is 'no', then don't do the same to them! Would you like it if others showed you respect? Of course, you do! So, try to show respect to others first. **You gain respect by giving respect.**

It is simply treating people the way you want to be treated. Doing so involves a lot of putting yourself in their shoes and a bit of your imagination. When you follow the Golden Rule and ask yourself, "Would I like it if someone acted like this to me?" it will not only improve your people skills, but your life in general. This is because, through showing kindness to other people, you will be more likely to receive a similar kindness back. If people are seeing that you are making an effort to show kindness and have a kind heart themselves, you will feel their compassion be reflected onto you.

Rule #30: To be a Good Speaker, You Must Be a Good Listener

One important thing to remember is that, people are naturally interested in themselves. Think about it: if your friend shows you a group photo that you are in, what is your first reaction? To find yourself in the photo! It's human nature to focus on the self, even when we try not to.

Using this fact can help you become a better conversationalist, because knowing that people care about themselves means that people are likely to enjoy talking about themselves as well. You should therefore give people the opportunity to speak about their lives, their hobbies and their passions and you should show interest when they do this.

In order to become interesting to others, you must first show that you are interested in them and have a willingness to listen to what they have to say. This does not mean you shouldn't have your own input in conversations, as it is important to talk about yourself also. It just means that you should give the person an opportunity to talk about their interests and show that you are engaged when they are.

Here is an example of a conversation where you are showing good listening skills and a strong interest in the other person. In this scenario, we have Gabriel and Sarah:

GABRIEL: "Hi Sarah! How have you been?

By asking an open question such as "how have you been?" or "how are you doing?" you are allowing for Sarah to talk about whatever may be on her mind at that moment. It also shows you are interested in what is going on in her life.

SARAH: "Hey Gabriel! I've just come back from shopping and I'm feeling a bit tired but apart from that everything is good! How about you?

Here, Sarah has told you what she was doing all day, told you she is feeling tired and then asked you how you are doing. Instead of talking for ages about yourself because she has asked about you, show that you have been listening to what she has said

GABRIEL: "I've been fine! Shopping can be a bit tiring especially when it's busy. What were you shopping for?

Responding in this way shows amazing listening skills. You made sure you answered Sarah's question but instead of taking the opportunity to talk for ages about yourself and what you have been up to, you have shown interest in the other person. Firstly, you showed empathy and understanding by **agreeing that shopping can be tiring**. You then showed interest by **asking more questions about her** and what she was specifically doing. Now Sarah can talk to you more about her day and you can find more opportunities to ask her questions from the information she gives.

In conversations, there will be plenty of time to talk about yourself later but at the start, show that you are interested in what the other person has to say. Eventually, the conversation will shift to you and what you want to talk about but showing interest towards them at the start is a great way for people to like you and want to talk to you more. Notice also that in the example, Sarah is not interrupted while she is speaking. Instead, she is shown the respect she needs while talking about herself.

Remember the last rule - "Treat others how you would like to be treated". Would you like it if someone interrupted you to talk about themselves for ages? It would not only be rude but would also bore you to death! So, don't do that to them!

Rule #31: People Will Remember How You Made Them Feel, Not What Was Said

Think about all the people you feel comfortable speaking to. Do you remember every conversation you've ever had with them? It's highly unlikely. You are more likely to enjoy speaking to these people because they made you feel good when you spoke to them in the past, either by acting warmly towards you or showing good listening skills.

Don't worry too much about trying to talk about the most interesting things in the world when you are in a conversation. Just show those amazing listening skills we discussed and try to be positive, confident and smile. **When you show you are trying to be kind and warm, people will enjoy talking to you, even if it is about boring topics such as the weather**. In the future, when you meet those people again, they won't remember what you were talking about, but they will remember that you made them feel warm and welcome.

Rule #32: Be Reliable

When I was a student many years ago, we went on a school trip to the London Stock Exchange. I remember very clearly seeing the words, "My word is my bond" written across the walls. When you give someone your word (promise), it means that you must do it whatever the circumstances. Breaking this bond means letting the person who trusted you down.

Being reliable means keeping the promises you make. In the same way, it means never making promises you can't fulfil. It is always better to admit that you can't do something than to pretend that you can and break your promise. Honesty is always the best policy when it comes to making promises. When you pretend you can make a promise you can't keep, you raise the hopes of the other person, only to disappoint them and let them down. This paints you as someone who is not only unreliable, but untrustworthy.

Remember, once again the Golden Rule, to "Treat others as you would like to be treated". Imagine how you would feel if somebody let you down. Don't do the same to others.

Rule #33: Be Generous and Charitable

One evening I was sitting on the tube on my way home from dinner with a friend. As we chatted away, the door opened and a young man with torn and dirty clothes entered the carriage. He apologised first and then announced to the passengers that he was 18 years old, homeless and hungry. In response, many of the people on the train ignored him.

Understanding the need for compassion and kindness, my friend and I searched our purses for change, only to find that we did not have any. After my friend left the carriage, I looked in the direction of the teenager and felt certain emptiness at the fact that I was unable to help him. I used the Golden Rule and put myself in the boy's shoes. It must have been difficult to endure what he was going through. It was soon to be my stop and I was one of the people on the carriage who failed to show compassion to the boy.

Impulsively, as the train slowed to the platform, I opened my wallet and took out a £10 note. I realised that, although it was more than I initially felt I should have given, it meant more to the homeless person than it did to me. I caught his attention as he walked past me and put the note in his hand. In response, he lunged forwards and gave me one of the smelliest hugs I have received in my life. The truth is that I did not care. I hugged him back understanding how difficult it must have been for him and how privileged I was to be able to go home and have a bath, whilst he had no home to go to. I told him to buy some food and take care of himself; I then left the train feeling better than when I entered it.

Giving more than you feel prepared to is a good example of generosity, which is a result of kindness and compassion. The feeling of love that you get from helping those who are unfortunate is worth more than the £10 in your wallet. Money isn't everything – at the end of the day **it is the good things we do for one another that counts.**

Be sure to help those less fortunate, whether you are giving them direct help or helping a charitable organisation. Sometimes it can be better to give to an organisation that knows what they're doing, as unfortunately not everybody who asks for help is honest about their situation. Use the Golden Rule and put yourself in the position of those who you are helping and realise how giving a little can help a lot.

Rule #34: Show Kindness and Compassion In More Ways Than One

Compassion means showing concern for the suffering and misfortune of others. Kindness is the quality of being generous and considerate. Both these qualities come hand in hand. In the previous rule, I emphasised the importance of generosity. Giving to charity is in itself an act of kindness and compassion but there are many situations in which you can show these traits without giving things physically. In some cases, you must weigh up what the best action is to take in order to show love to the most people.

When I was in my early teens, on my way home, I came across an old man sleeping on the pavement. He was thin, frail and unbathed. What struck me most were the tattered rags he draped around himself as clothes. They were torn and dirty and clearly overused. I ran home and gathered most of my late grandfather's clothes in a bag. I walked confidently out of the house and gave the sack to the homeless man I had walked by earlier, who took the charity and left. In that moment I was proud of myself for taking the initiative to help this man but as I came home, I saw my grandmother sad and in tears.

My grandparents had been married since she was 18 and the clothes I had given away were kept so she could remember her late husband. After realising what I had done, I broke down into tears and apologised, explaining that I was only trying to help. She quickly forgave me and told me she loved me.

Although it is important to give generously, it is also important to think about the feelings of others around you. The clothes I had given were not mine to give and had sentimental value to my grandma. Although my intentions were good, they still had a bad effect on how she felt. Sometimes it is appropriate to show compassion through performing other kind acts, such as having a conversation with somebody who is lonely or helping someone who is lost find their way. In this situation it would have been best to talk to my grandma before I acted. Maybe then we could have helped the homeless man together in a way that would have not hurt her feelings.

Rule #35: Return What Does Not Belong To You

I am sure you have heard of the overused phrase, "Finders keepers." If you haven't, it is a term used to justify keeping something that doesn't belong to you, simply because you are the person who found it.

I can recall one morning, not too long ago that I found a beautiful pair of designer sunglasses on the bus that took me to work. It would have been easy to claim the pair on my own simply because "Finders keepers" however, I took a second to think about the Golden Rule. I put myself in the other person's shoes and immediately thought about the owner, frantically searching for where she put them last. Instead of pocketing the goods, I realised that the lady who lost the glasses may return in search for them, given how expensive they were and so on my way off the bus, I handed the pair to the driver and requested he give them to lost property.

We must do what we can to return the things that are lost to their rightful owner. Only then should you be able to keep something that is not yours. Doing so before you have attempted to return them is essentially stealing.

Rule #36: Ensure That Others Return What Is Rightfully Yours

In the same way that you should return things to other people, you should always ensure that you are given back what is yours. Sometimes, people can make the mistake of letting someone they think they trust borrow something from them. They can then soon realise that person is not as trustworthy as they thought and it can be difficult to get what they offered back.

Only ever give to those you love and trust and if your trust is ever betrayed and someone keeps something that is not theirs after trying to reclaim it and failing, learn your lesson and be more cautious of whom you find trustworthy.

Generosity is good, but some people don't deserve it if they are untrustworthy.

Rule #37: Forgive But Never Forget

This life is full of people who may do you wrong. It may be a stranger or a friend or even a family member. When this happens, try to learn to forgive them for your own sake. Holding a grudge (being upset and resentful and having hatred play in your mind) feels like carrying a heavy weight around wherever you go.

It is important to forgive others for their misdoings. Ultimately, **nobody is perfect and forgiveness is the first step to improving yourself emotionally. The key thing to remember once forgiveness is given, however, is to never forget the lesson you learned.** You can forgive someone without allowing them to do the same horrible thing again.

Rule #38: Be Honest But Discreet

So far, I've mentioned a lot of famous phrases about life. One of my personal favourites is "Honesty is the best policy." It is often the case that those who live an honest life have it much easier than those who don't. One lie can often lead to another until you find yourself caught in a tangled web of the stuff.

Honesty means telling someone when you can't do something or admitting to when you have done something wrong. It also means speaking out when you feel that something wrong is happening. It is important to be honest in life as it means you are comfortable with who you are and are not out to mislead people. It is sometimes the case; however, that honesty can conflict with the need to be discreet.

As important as it is to give your honest opinion, it is even more important to make sure that you have been asked for it. This is because giving your honest opinion to someone who has not asked for it can come across as rude.

An example of this is if you think someone is wearing something does not fit them. If the person asked you, "Do you think what I'm wearing looks a bit tight?" then you should be able to tell them, "In all honesty, I think it looks a little tight fitting. Maybe you can try on something that suits you better?" Now imagine you walk up to a stranger and tell them that you think they look silly in what they're wearing. Do you think that stranger would appreciate your opinion? Instead of thanking you they would think you are being rude.

When you were about 5 years old, I took you to one of my friend's birthday parties. Whilst at this event, one of the guests noticed that you acted slightly differently from the other children in the way you interacted with them. Instead of keeping her observations to herself, she felt the need to express them in front of everyone who was there and asked me if you were autistic.

In this example, the lady did not have an awareness of the need to be discreet. Although she may have told me what she honestly thought, there was no need for her to say it as it wasn't an appropriate question, nor was it the right place or time to ask.

I later took her aside and told her that asking sensitive questions in public was inconsiderate and she apologised immediately. It is easy to think something and feel the need to say it out loud but this is not a good use of honesty. Instead it is careless behaviour. **Be mindful of what you say to others and be discreet when necessary.**

Rule #39: Don't Overestimate Your Ability To Change Others

There will often be times when you see flaws in other people and feel that you can help them be better. There will be times you will want other people to change. The truth is that people are the way that they are for many reasons and you cannot control their thoughts or their actions. Trying to do so will just leave you disappointed.

It is ultimately up to the people themselves whether they want to change. Of course, you may give advice to others if done in a way that isn't rude, but the important thing is to not be surprised if your advice is not followed. **It is difficult to change the behaviours of other people. At the end of the day, you are the only one who can be changed by you.**

Rule #40: Patience Is A Virtue

Good things take time. Sometimes, life may get in the way and they can take more time than you would expect. Halfway through writing this rulebook, I forgot the password to access my work. I attempted to enter the document for hours, but I was unsuccessful in the end.

I could have gotten so angry with myself and decided to quit, but instead I started again from scratch. The process took a lot of patience and without this patience, the book you are reading would not be in your hands. Oftentimes it is important to try again even if the process takes up your time because at the end of the hard work, there are good results.

Patience runs through most aspects of your life. When you find yourself slowly getting angry or desperate, just remember that patience will get you through it. If someone is difficult to deal with or finds it hard to understand you, have patience with them. Things will always change over time. Things will always get better if you let them. Don't rush everything along.

Rule #41: Don't Fight Fire With Fire

This phrase is used a lot, but what does it mean?

When another person is enraged or angry, the proper way to respond is not to match their anger. Have you ever seen an argument between two angry people? Does it get anywhere? No! It simply escalates and explodes.

Instead of shouting back or responding in a mad rage, **remember that remaining calm wins the argument.** Choosing not to fight back and taking the diplomatic and intelligent approach makes the other person seem insane. If you take the bait and respond in a similar manner, the whole situation will simply go in flames and there will be no solution to the problem. Control your emotions.

Rule #42: Learn How To Say No (Politely)

There will be times that people ask you to do things that you cannot and do not want to do. Don't try to be a people pleaser. If you know you are unable to fulfil a task, simply decline it politely. Saying yes to everything will always set you up for disappointment as you cannot please everybody you know. It will also mean you end up wasting a lot of your time doing things that you do not want to do.

Here are some examples of how to politely decline a request:

Person May Say…	Politely Declining
"Come to my party Gabriel. There will be a lot of food and you will have fun."	"I hope you have a lovely night, but unfortunately, I can't come this evening because I'm quite busy."
(Over the phone) "Hi! Is this Gabriel? We want to save you a great deal of money on your utility bills."	"Sorry, but I am not interested in this call and don't know how you got my number. Can you please refrain from calling again? Thank you!"

Saying no is most important when you are feeling pressured into something. It takes a lot of courage to tell another person that you don't want to do something under pressure but people will respect you more if you stick to your morals rather than just saying yes to seem cool. If anybody ever tries to pressure you into doing something, simply say:

"Sorry, I don't feel comfortable doing what you're asking me to do. Hopefully you can respect that."

If the other person persists aggressively, then they are the ones who are now being rude and you have the right to make it as clear as you want that the answer is no.

Learning to say no is important but remember that in certain situations someone may be trying to help you and it is up to you to decide whether saying yes is something you want to do or not. Make sure you follow the previous rules and use your listening skills before you decide to say no.

Rule #43: Give People More Than One Option

It always helps to give people options when deciding on something. Doing this shows that you value their decisions and are willing to listen to them, as well as giving the other person a greater sense of control.

For example, you call your best friend and ask "Hey, should we meet up for lunch? I'm free at any time between 11am and 4pm. If not, I'll be free on Wednesday." You are giving them options as to when they can meet you. This is much better than simply deciding the time they should see you and shows that you are considerate. It also means that you are more likely to see this person as if they cannot make the times you stated, they have the option to see you on another day that may suit them.

Giving people a choice is an important part of communication and shows that you don't think the world revolves around you. There will be times that a person will not be able to choose and may ask you to choose for them. There will also be times that the choices you have given them are not enough. Be prepared for either outcome and remember that you can't control other people (See **Rule #39**).

Rule #44: Always Clarify

Have you ever been in a position where someone tells you something but you haven't fully understood what they have said? You might feel embarrassed to show that you didn't understand but remember it is always important to clarify.

Clarifying ensures you follow instructions correctly and are less likely to make mistakes. People will be significantly less likely to get annoyed with you if you ask for clarification than if you go ahead and carry out a task incorrectly. There are several ways in which you can clarify something.

Usually the best way to do it is to:

1) State that you aren't too sure about something.
2) Explain what you have understood so far to demonstrate that you were listening.

Here's an easy example in which someone is trying to explain how to make tea. Imagine they have gone through all the steps, but you don't quite remember them:

1) Make it clear that you aren't too sure about something by saying "Sorry, but I didn't really understand what you said."
2) Explain what you have understood: "I know that I should boil the water first and add it to the tea bag, but I'm confused about the amount of milk and sugar I should use. Can you run through it again?"

Sometimes, you might not have understood anything that was said at all. If this is the case, simply say

   "I am sorry, but I didn't get it. Can you say it again for me please and simplify it a little?"

Clarifying demonstrates willingness to understand. People respect it when someone has the courage to ask for clarification rather than do something wrongly out of fear of asking.

Rule #45: Don't Take More Than You Give and Don't Give More Than You Take

All relationships involve an element of give and take. If you love someone, you should be willing to give generously to them. But if they love you, they should also be willing to do the same. The idea of a relationship is that things should be balanced between the two people.

If you feel that you are taking too much from a relationship, tell the other person that you want to treat them. Similarly, if you feel you are giving too much in a relationship, make sure you understand why that is. It is easy for people to get used to being pampered and taking advantage of another person's love. You need to make sure that the other person is not taking advantage of you; otherwise the relationship will turn sour.

This concept not only applies to romantic relationships. It also doesn't only apply to money and materialistic things either. It can apply to friendships as well and the commodity of time. If you feel that you are giving a lot of your time and energy to someone, but they will not do the same to you, then that is an unhealthy relationship. The way to address it is to either give less or tell the person they are not giving enough and explain why you feel that way. A good partner will try and understand you and be better because of their love and respect for you.

Rule #46: For the Boys - Be a Gentleman

Being chivalrous is an old-fashioned way of saying being a gentleman. We live in a world today where we value equality and the need for men and women to be treated the same. As shown in the last rule, there is a need for relationships to be balanced and equal. Even still, this does not mean that the act of being a gentleman does not exist.

Being chivalrous (or a gentleman) means showing respect to women and treating them right. It is right for the person who asked someone out on a date to pay for the other person. Unfortunately, girls often wait for guys to make the first move and so it is unlikely that they would be the first to initiate.

Remember that money is not everything and a small thing like offering to pay for the other person's food will be seen as kind and generous. It also means that you will most likely have future dates with the other person, where they may treat you or you may share the bill.

Remember that being chivalrous is more than just paying for someone's meal. **It is the act of showing respect to women and treating them kindly**. Simple gestures such as opening a door for someone and respecting personal space are good ways of showing how gentleman-like you are.

Rule #47: Don't Be Afraid Of Rejection

I mentioned earlier the story of Colonel Sanders, the man who created KFC. He was rejected over 1,000 times before finding someone who accepted his recipe for fried chicken. He then went on to have the largest and fastest growing fried chicken company in the world.

The same rule applies to not only life but your approach to relationships. If you ever find yourself liking someone and spending a lot of time with them and you feel that they may feel the same way about you, don't be afraid to properly ask them out on a date. It takes a lot of courage but getting a yes or a no, will benefit you, as you will learn whether that person is on the same page as you or not.

If the answer is yes, then great! If it's a no, then that's also good, as you can move on and look for someone else who will be interested in having your friendship.

Rule #48: Ask Questions

Asking questions is one of the best ways to get to know another human being. It shows others that you are interested in them and listening to what they have to say. It also shows that you have an intelligent and inquisitive mind.

Don't ever be afraid to ask questions but ensure that the questions you are asking are appropriate. Keeping in mind what I mentioned earlier in this book about being discreet, don't ask questions that may be too sensitive or questions that may offend the other person. Instead, **ask people about their interests and hobbies, or their thoughts and opinions.**

The easiest way to hold a conversation is to have a back and forth of ideas and questions. Sometimes they may ask you something and other times it can work the other way. Ultimately, you will be sharing information about each other and this can make for a good and interesting conversation.

Rule #49: Don't Be Afraid To Open Up To People

Lots of people tend to find it difficult to open up. By this, I mean it is often hard to talk about your inner thoughts, feelings, dreams and fears. Opening up doesn't mean telling someone all your secrets, but it means you can tell someone things about you that are more intimate than small talk. Of course, it is great to tell people what you are good at (as long as you aren't bragging) and talk about the things you enjoy but it is even better to admit the things you find challenging or the things that scare you in life.

Telling someone that you have autism is an example of opening up. It is something personal to you that may present with challenges and gifts. **It is a declaration that may help other people to understand you better and be more mindful in their interactions with you**. In some cases, it may even be something that another person has in common with you, in which case sharing this can help form a bond between you and that other person.

The key is to open up to people only if you feel you can trust them and you feel comfortable doing so. Don't ever feel like it is something that is forced. Although opening up can make you feel vulnerable at times, it can also strengthen your relationship with others as you are sharing things that have meaning to you.

Rule #50: Seek Guidance When You Are Lost, For You Are Never Alone

People often make the mistake of trying to do things all by themselves. **It is admirable to be independent but even more to seek help when necessary.** I wrote these rules for you as one of the many things you can turn to when you are feeling lost and alone. In here lies the majority of my wisdom on how to lead a happy life.

This last rule is the most important of them all. It ensures you will use this advice when you find yourself in difficult times. It also serves as a reminder that you are never alone. Even when you feel you are, there are communities out there to help you. There are books out there to read. Most importantly, you have the power of prayer to guide you whenever you feel truly alone, for God is always listening.

As a final note to my son, Gabriel. I have written these 50 Rules primarily for you, so that my voice is forever locked in these pages to guide you. I want you to know that even when I am not physically by your side, you have my words and wisdom to read through for guidance. I believe you will have an amazing life and that God will make a way for you, as long as your heart is in the right place.

ACKNOWLEDGEMENTS

From the bottom of my heart, a million thanks to the following:

Vicente Majaba – My beloved husband for your love and support.

Zinedine Afir – My wonderful nephew who edited this book. I would never have done it without your help.

Marlon Pempengco – My darling nephew who helped me upload this book on Amazon website.

Virda Pempengco – My beloved sister who tirelessly encouraged me to write this book.

And finally to:

Jennifer Viloria – My beautiful best friend whose encouragement I will never forget. Our friendship has stood the test of time.

www.ingramcontent.com/pod-product-compliance
Lightning Source LLC
Chambersburg PA
CBHW042044110726
48006CB00002B/288